POLLUTION:

the NOISE
we hear

The Real World Books
on
Pollution

THE WATERS OF THE EARTH

THE AIR WE BREATHE

THE LAND WE LIVE ON

THE DANGEROUS ATOM

THE NOISE WE HEAR

THE FOOD WE EAT

THE BALANCE OF NATURE

THE POPULATION EXPLOSION

**These books are printed on
paper containing recycled fiber.**

POLLUTION:

the NOISE we hear

Claire Jones
Steve J. Gadler
Paul H. Engstrom

LERNER PUBLICATIONS COMPANY
Minneapolis, Minnesota

Acknowledgments

The illustrations are reproduced through the courtesy of: p. 6, *Minneapolis Tribune*; pp. 9, 56, 58, 64, 76, United States Department of Commerce, National Bureau of Standards; pp. 27, 36, 53, 67, Nancy Bundt; p. 30 (bottom), United Nations; p. 34, Federal Reserve Bank of New York; pp. 39, 42, 45, 54, 84, Independent Picture Service; p. 46, Bethlehem Steel Corporation; pp. 48, 79, Central Foundry, Division of General Motors; p. 60 (top and bottom), General Motors Corporation; pp. 62, 71, Henry Valiukas; p. 73, Con Edison; p. 81, National Environmental Instruments, Inc.; p. 88, Harshe-Rotman & Druck, Inc.; p. 90, Citizens for a Quieter City.

The Library of Congress cataloged the
original printing of this title as follows:

Jones, Claire.
  Pollution: the noise we hear [by] Claire Jones, Steve J. Gadler [and] Paul H. Engstrom. Minneapolis, Lerner Publications Co. [1972]

  95 p. illus. 23 cm. (A Real World Book)

  SUMMARY: Examines the physical and psychological effects of noise and the controls that would eliminate damaging factors.

  1. Noise pollution—Juvenile literature. [1. Noise pollution]
I. Gadler, Steve J., joint author. II. Engstrom, Paul H., joint author. III. Title.

TD892.J65 1972	620.2'3	79-165323
ISBN 0-8225-0631-9		MARC
		AC

International Standard Book Number: 0-8225-0631-9
Library of Congress Catalog Card Number: 79-165323

Second Printing 1972

Contents

8455

Noise pollution is a major problem in many metropolitan areas. The inhabitants of our crowded cities are threatened by the high levels of noise which are part of their daily lives.

1

Assault on our Ears

Thirteen-year-old Roy Innis lay dead on the sidewalk in front of an apartment building in the Bronx. Only minutes earlier he had been happily shouting, racing, and wrestling with his brother and two friends. Roy had been shot and killed by a man trying to sleep in one of the second floor apartments, a man who had been driven to distraction by the noise the boys were making. As the angry neighbor came downstairs with his pistol, the boys started to run. Roy was killed by a shot that struck him in the back.

When a new flight path brought low-flying military jets directly over his home near Munich, Germany, artist Helmut Winter complained to the authorities. But the flights continued. Infuriated by the persistent noise, Winter set to work building a modern version of the Roman ballista, a device which projected missiles in the manner of a greatly enlarged slingshot. For his projectiles Winter used potato dumplings, aiming them at the fuselages of the low-flying planes. Striking with a solid "plop, plop, plop," the dumplings caused such frightening vibrations throughout the aircraft that the flight path was changed to avoid them, and Winter's life became peaceful once again.

Like Helmut Winter and Roy Innis, people over the centuries have learned that noise can be both annoying and destructive. Two thousand years ago the Chinese used noise as a device to torture and punish criminals. The culprits were forced to listen to the noise of bells ringing loudly, without interruption; they first went insane and then died. In the first century B.C., Julius Caesar tackled the problem of traffic noise in Rome by banning chariots from the cobblestone streets at night because the noise they made was disturbing the Romans' sleep.

In our living, breathing, moving world, noise is all around us. What can you hear now, this minute? Birds singing? The soft chords of a guitar? Traffic noise? The pounding of feet in a hallway? Voices cheering your team to victory? The whine of a jet? Your next-door neighbors arguing?

Sound is an important part of our everyday lives. It is a form of communication by which we exchange thoughts and feelings. It calls forth all kinds of emotional responses, ranging through many levels of pleasure, indifference, annoyance, fury, or even physical pain. We each react to sounds in our own individual way, depending on what the sounds mean to us personally. When sound is unwanted, we call it noise. Some sounds are universally disliked—for instance, the screech of a jackhammer or the rattle of

The screech of a jackhammer is one of the most unpopular noises heard in our city streets today.

a riveting gun. But often the distinction between pleasurable sound and unwanted noise is purely a subjective one, varying from one person to another and from one time and place to another.

During most of the day, a bird song is a pretty and welcome sound. But in the early hours of a summer dawn the chirping and twittering of birds can be an irritating noise which disturbs our sleep. Speech can be a friendly and useful sound, telling us things we want to hear. But the harsh yak of a voice which never stops soon becomes unwanted noise. When we are waiting at an airport for someone we love, the whine of an approaching jet can seem an exciting and welcome sound. But to thousands of people living nearby, that same whine from that same jet is an infuriating noise.

Music in all its wide variety of sound causes widely differing reactions. In this area perhaps more than any other, one man's delight is another man's horror. We may dig the mind-blowing hard rock at our own parties, but the late-night frenzy of a neighbor's party makes a noise that we prefer to do without. Most people have very definite ideas about when and where they want to hear music. When the English playwright George Bernard Shaw went into a famous London restaurant, he was treated with great deference by the headwaiter, who said to him, "While you are eating, the orchestra will play anything you like. What would you like them to play?" Shaw replied, "Dominoes."

Shaw was able to make a choice about the sounds he would hear, but most of us are not so fortunate. Our lives are filled with all kinds of noise, and much of it is potentially damaging. It can hurt our bodies and our minds. It can hurt the other living creatures with whom we share this planet. It can destroy nonliving things made of metal and glass. As the noise levels in our crowded society rise higher and higher, we face increasing problems of noise pollution. Before we look more closely at some of these problems, let us think a little about the nature of sound itself.

2

The Anatomy of Sound

The source of sound is a vibrating object such as a tuning fork, a guitar string, a drill tearing at concrete, or the vocal chords of people and animals. When an object vibrates to and fro, it causes the surrounding air to vibrate by compressing and then expanding the air molecules. As the object moves in one direction, it compresses the molecules closest to it. These compressed molecules in turn push against the next molecules, causing them to squeeze together. The same thing happens to the next group of molecules, and the next, and so on. Meanwhile, the vibrating object has moved back again, past its original position and on to the other side. It leaves behind an empty space into which the original compressed molecules expand. The molecules next to them also expand in their turn, and the next, and so on. The areas of expansion alternate with the areas of compression, spreading outward from the vibrating object like the ripples created when a rock is thrown into a pool of water.

Each time the object vibrates to and fro, it creates a new series of compressions and expansions, which move through the surrounding air in the form of a pressure wave. When sound waves strike a soft surface, like fabric drapes or foam insulating material, they are absorbed and deadened. When they strike a hard surface, like concrete walls or steel panels, the sound bounces off, is reflected and scattered. If sound waves are not deflected or absorbed, they continue to spread until the energy that propels them is used up. Then they fade away.

The sounds of our noisy world, then, are actually vibrations that enter our ears and are interpreted by our brains. Most of the sounds we hear travel to us through the air. But sound waves can also travel in similar and often more efficient ways by disturbing the molecules of other substances. A substance's ability to conduct sound increases with its density; thus solids are better conductors than liquids, or gases such as air. With your ear to the ground you can hear the thud of horses' hooves at much greater distances than you can hear the same sound when it travels through the air. When you are standing beside someone, you cannot hear his heart beating. But lay your ear to his chest or listen through a stethoscope, and you can hear the sound waves quite clearly.

Sound cannot travel at all when there is no medium for it to pass through. Without a medium, there are no molecules which can be set in motion by a vibration. Therefore, sound waves will not travel through a vacuum or through outer space, where the scattered molecules of air are too far apart to be built up into waves.

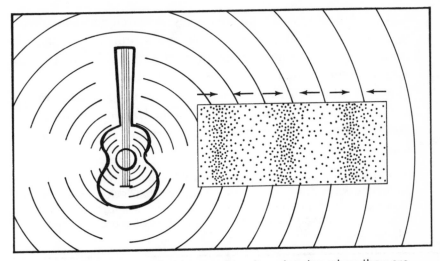

This drawing shows what happens to air molecules when they are set in motion by a vibrating object. When the string of the guitar begins to vibrate, moving from left to right, it compresses the air molecules in the direction in which it is moving. When the string moves back in the opposite direction, the compressed molecules expand. The alternating areas of compression and expansion form sound waves which spread outward in all directions as the string continues to vibrate. (Here we see only one small area of molecules greatly enlarged.)

Sound waves have different characteristics, which enable us to distinguish one kind of sound from another. The sounds that we hear vary in *pitch*, which can be loosely defined as the relative highness or lowness of a sound. The thunk of a wooden door closing, for instance, has a lower sound than the clink of ice in a glass. Pitch is determined by the *frequency* of a sound wave—the rapidity with which it vibrates. A sound that is pitched high on the scale is carried by short sound waves which are close together and vibrate rapidly. A low note on the scale is produced by long sound waves which are far apart and vibrate slowly. Sound frequency is usually measured in cycles per second. (A cycle is one vibration, or one compression and one expansion of the molecules of the sound-carrying medium.) Thus, the highest note on a piano vibrates at 4,000 cycles per second, the lowest note at 27 cycles per second. A high-pitched sound with its fast vibrations seems to be more penetrating and to cause more annoyance than one of a lower pitch.

A low-frequency sound wave has a longer wave length than a high-frequency wave. It vibrates more slowly, so that fewer vibrations pass a given point in a period of time. Sound waves of low frequency produce low-pitched sounds; high-frequency waves produce high-pitched sounds.

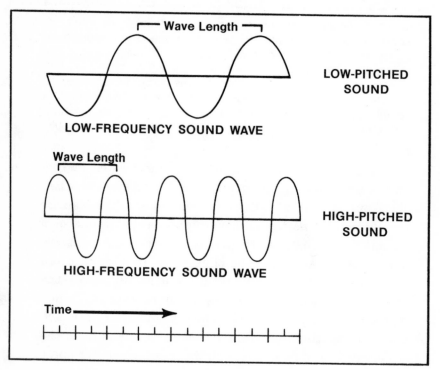

One of the properties of sound which affects us most directly is its *intensity*, that is, the amount of energy or power flowing in the sound waves. When a sound wave reaches our ears, its intensity is translated into *loudness*, which can be defined as the strength of the sensation that the sound produces. Although they are closely related, intensity and loudness are not quite the same thing. The loudness of a sound depends not only on its intensity but also on its frequency; the higher the frequency, the louder the sound will seem, even though the intensity has not been changed. Also, people vary a great deal in their reactions to a sound of the same intensity. What may seem comfortable to one person can seem loud, almost to the threshold of pain, to another.

Since loudness depends to some extent on individual perception of a sound, it is difficult to measure. However, the measurement of sound intensity is one of the most important tools that acoustical scientists and engineers use in their work. Intensity is measured by an electronic device called a sound level meter and is most commonly expressed in *decibels*, often abbreviated to dB. The decibel unit is named after Alexander Graham Bell, a sound researcher who invented the telephone and also did valuable work with deaf people. The decibel scale was devised to measure the smallest difference in sound which is detectable by the human ear. Its gradations move up not in a simple arithmetic progression but in a multiple progression based on logarithmic calculations. This means that each increase of one decibel represents a much larger change of intensity than might be expected. For example: If we add five oranges to a carton which already contains 100 oranges, then we are adding, by simple arithmetic

Noise	Decibels
THRESHOLD OF AUDIBILITY	0
RUSTLING LEAVES	20
SOFT WHISPER 5 FEET AWAY	30
CONVERSATION	60
VACUUM CLEANER	75
RINGING ALARM CLOCK	80
GARBAGE COLLECTION	85
HEAVY CITY TRAFFIC	92
POWER SAW	98
NOISY FACTORY	100
RIVETER	115
JET AIRLINER 100 FEET AWAY	140

DECIBELS: 0 10 20 30 40 50 60 70 80 90 100 110 120 130 140

SOUND LEVEL READINGS FOR SOME COMMON NOISES

progression, just 5 percent, or 1/20, more oranges. But because of the logarithmic progression of the decibel scale, an increase of five decibels means that sound intensity has increased by about *100* percent. A sound which measures 105 decibels on a sound level meter is more than *twice as intense* as one which measures 100 decibels. This is a very important point to remember when comparing the intensity of one sound with that of another.

A sound that registers 0 dBs on the decibel scale is the quietest sound that a healthy human ear is capable of hearing; it is said to be at the threshold of audibility. A sound of 10 dBs—for instance, the sound of a pin dropping on a hard surface—is 10 times louder than a sound of 0 dBs. The sound of rustling leaves has an intensity of about 20 dBs, which is 100 times louder than 0 dBs. A whisper heard from five feet away might register 30 dBs on a sound level meter. This would be 1,000 times louder than 0 dBs.

Specialized variations of the decibel scale include perceived noise-level in decibels (PNdB), which takes into account pitch and quality of sound; effective perceived noise-level (EPNdB), which includes adjustments for pitch and duration; and noise level in the A scale of frequencies (dB-A), the scale to which the human ear is most sensitive.

Most otologists (ear specialists) believe that prolonged exposure to noise measuring 85 decibels or more results in damage to the hearing mechanism. Physical discomfort is experienced when noise reaches 120 decibels; this level on the decibel scale is known as the threshold of feeling. At 140 decibels the discomfort changes to physical pain. Mechanical damage to inanimate things begins at noise levels of 155 decibels.

There are many variations in the levels of sound intensity, as there are in the other characteristics of sound such as frequency, amplitude, and pitch. However, the speed of sound moving through air is relatively constant, varying only in relation to differences in temperature at different altitudes. (Colder temperatures lower the density and therefore the elasticity of air, and decreased elasticity slows down the movement of sound waves.) The normal speed of sound in air at sea level is 1,100 feet per second, or about 760 miles per hour.

When an object moves faster than the speed of sound, it causes an intense disturbance of the air around it. In the case of a supersonic aircraft, this disturbance produces the complicated phenomenon known as a *sonic boom*. The speed of a moving plane in relation to the speed of sound is usually measured in Mach numbers, named after the 19th-century Austrian physicist Ernst Mach. A plane flying at the speed of sound is said to be flying at Mach 1; Mach 2 is twice the speed of sound, and so on. When an aircraft travels more slowly than the speed of sound, that is, at speeds under Mach 1, it creates pressure waves of sound which move ahead of it. The waves set up patterns of movement which, in a sense, prepare the air molecules for the plane's passage. However, when a plane moves at supersonic speeds, it moves *faster* than the sound waves it is creating. The molecules of air in the airplane's path receive no warning of its approach. As a result, the plane slams into the mass of air molecules in front of it, creating shock waves of compressed air. The shock waves formed at the plane's nose, at its wings, and at the tail combine in a cone-shaped wave that encircles the plane and trails

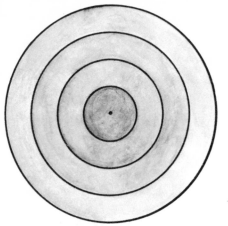

UNDERSTANDING
THE SONIC BOOM

Sound spreads from a stationary source in concentric spheres.

This diagram shows sound spreading from a source moving at subsonic speeds. When the source is at position 1, it produces the sphere of sound labeled 1; sphere 2 is produced at position 2, and so on. Because the source is in motion, it does not remain at the center of its spheres of sound. But because it is traveling more slowly than the speed of sound, it will never get ahead of the sound waves it is creating.

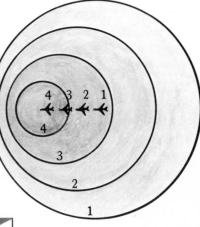

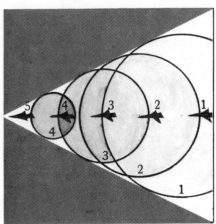

When the source of sound is moving at supersonic speeds, it moves faster than the sound waves it produces. At position 5, the supersonic plane in the diagram has left all of its spheres of sound behind and is slamming into masses of air molecules unprepared for its passage. The resulting shock wave of compressed air produces the sonic boom.

behind it. When the trailing edge of the cone strikes the ground, it creates the familiar thunder-crack sound of the sonic boom. A supersonic plane lays down a continuous boom "carpet" from 50 to 80 miles wide, all along the path of its flight. Anyone living in this area will be subjected to the annoyance of the sonic boom.

Regardless of their intensity, sounds such as the sonic boom will not be heard unless they fall within a certain range of frequencies. The normal human ear can hear sound waves which vibrate at frequencies between 15 cycles per second and 20,000 cycles per second. Sound which vibrates at frequencies over 20,000 cycles per second is known as *ultrasound.* Dogs can hear some of these higher frequencies and will come running in response to an ultrasonic whistle which is completely inaudible to the human ear. Horses, too, can hear some ultrasonic sounds. Dolphins are believed to communicate with each other by using some kind of ultrasonic "speech." Bats find their way by making ultrasonic sounds and then listening for the echoes which bounce back when the sound waves strike solid objects.

Although human beings cannot hear ultrasound, they have been able to put it to work for them. Submarines send out beams of ultrasonic sound which bounce back from objects under the water in the form of echoes. These echoes can be used to detect the location of other vessels or to measure the depth of the ocean. (This kind of ultrasonic sound system is called sonar, short for "sound navigation and ranging.") Industry uses ultrasonic detectors to find flaws in metal parts and in railroad tracks. Ultrasound is also used to kill insects and to pasteurize milk by killing bacteria. It is offensive to rats and other rodents and is used in flour mills to keep these pests away.

Sound with waves which vibrate at less than 15 cycles per second is called *infrasound*. It also is inaudible to human beings and, so far as we know, to other living creatures. Infrasound can be produced electronically and sensed by electronic instruments. France has been conducting military research on an acoustic weapon which sends out vibrations of less than 10 cycles per second. Although the vibrations cannot be heard, they create a pendulum action within the body, building up to unbearable intensities. During experiments on the infrasound weapon, some researchers have suffered intense pain in the stomach, the heart, and the lungs. Although few details have been made public yet, it seems likely that infrasound is also the basis for a new riot control device which has recently been patented in the United States. The noise is made electronically and beamed through reflectors, and is so distressing that hearers are forced to run from it.

Human beings are not equipped to hear the extremes of ultrasound and infrasound, but all other frequencies of sound register on the human ear and are intrepreted by the brain. The outer ear is the collecting point for the pattern of sound vibrations which reach us from our environment. These vibrations enter the ear and strike the thin membrane of the eardrum, which pulsates and activates three tiny bones in the middle ear. These delicate bones, called the hammer, the anvil, and the stirrup, convert the waves of airborne sound into waves in the fluid of the *cochlea*, a coiled tube in the inner ear which contains the organ of hearing. The waves in turn stimulate specialized sense cells which send nerve impulses to the

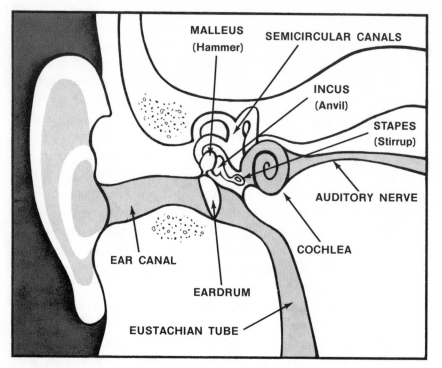

The structure of the human ear. The Eustachian tube connects the middle ear with the mouth and nose. The semicircular canals are organs of balance unrelated to the hearing mechanism.

brain. It is only when the brain has interpreted these impulses that the process of hearing is complete.

Within the complex hearing mechanism of the inner ear are microscopic fibers and hair cells, each of which responds only to a specific frequency. The ear must sort out millions of tones which combine to give a sound its meaning. Most human beings, as they grow older, gradually lose part of the efficiency of their hearing mechanism without being aware that it is fading. Only when we begin to have difficulty sorting out precise sounds such as speech do we realize that we are becoming deaf.

3

The Dangers of Noise

Damage to Living Things

For centuries people have assumed that deafness was part of the normal process of growing old. But now an increasing number of scientific tests are producing evidence that the deafness which comes with age is actually caused by the noise which continually bombards our ears.

Many years ago, Thomas Edison predicted that if urban noise continued to increase as it was doing then, modern man might evolve into a creature that is born deaf. More recently, Dr. Louis Freeman, a medical research director, said, "If city noise continues to rise as it has been rising— which is at the rate of one or more decibels per year— everyone will be stone deaf by the year 2000."

In the United States today, noise pollution is costing industry as much as $4 billion a year through time lost on the job and through payments of workmen's compensation for illness, deafness, and other physical damage caused by noise. The Veterans Administration spends $8 million a year on the claims of 5,000 servicemen whose hearing has been damaged by the noise of weapons. Around $65 million a year goes for rehabilitation programs to help 90,000 veterans who suffered hearing damage in the service.

It is apparent that many Americans have already fallen victim to the destructive force of noise. Others are being hurt by noise and do not know it. The deafness caused by noise pollution is insidious: it sneaks up on us so gradually that we do not realize how much hearing we have lost until it has gone forever. The effects of continuing loud noise are cumulative—they build up over a period of time. Eventually they cause a wearing away of the microscopic hair cells in the ears, which play such a vital part in transmitting sound to the brain. Cells which do not recover when the noise stops disintegrate completely. A single loud blast, such as the noise of a cannon, can destroy many of them irreparably. Loud noise is also known to cause a constriction of the tiny blood vessels in the body. Thus Dr. Samuel Rosen, a leading ear surgeon and auditory researcher in New York City, believes that continued exposure to excessive noise might eventually lead to a chronic state of blood deprivation in the inner ear and finally to the death of the cells involved in hearing.

The middle ear contains muscles which react automatically to protect the inner ear from excessive noise. When an intense noise occurs, the muscles contract, tightening the eardrum and the tiny bones in the middle ear. This action prevents the full force of the vibrations

24

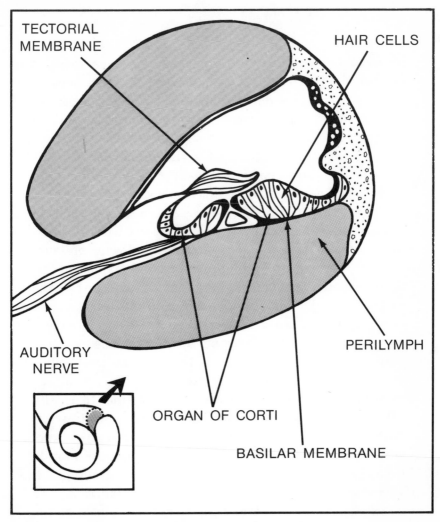

TECTORIAL MEMBRANE

HAIR CELLS

AUDITORY NERVE

PERILYMPH

ORGAN OF CORTI

BASILAR MEMBRANE

CROSS SECTION OF THE COCHLEA

The *basilar membrane* forms a partition that runs the length of the cochlea's coiled tube. Lying on top of the basilar membrane is the *organ of Corti*, a collection of fleshy cells which make up the human organ of hearing. Another membrane, the *tectorial membrane*, lies over the organ of Corti like a flap. The tiny *hair cells* embedded in the organ of Corti receive the vibrations of sound transmitted through the *perilymph*, the fluid which fills the cochlea. The hair cells transform the vibrations into nerve impulses which reach the brain by means of the *auditory nerve*. If the hair cells are damaged or destroyed, then hearing is permanently impaired.

from being transmitted to the inner ear. But these muscles can become weakened by too much use so that they are no longer capable of diminishing loud noise. People whose protective ear muscles remain strong usually keep acute hearing later in life than do people with weakened muscles.

The eardrum is another part of the human ear which is vulnerable to noise pollution. The strong vibrations of a sudden loud noise can cause excess blood to be sent to the eardrum; this reaction produces intense pain and in extreme cases may cause the eardrum to bleed. The eardrum can also be ruptured by violent sound-wave pressure such as that caused by big guns or bomb explosions. If the bones of the middle ear are not damaged, then the eardrum usually heals and some hearing returns.

A very loud noise or explosion can cause not only these varying degrees of permanent damage but also a more noticeable temporary loss of hearing. Immediately after being exposed to a loud noise, we find it difficult to hear moderate sounds such as normal conversation. It usually takes several hours for our ears and brains to readjust.

In an effort to discover the temporary effects of exposure to loud noise, researchers at the University of Florida College of Medicine tested the hearing of a group of 14-year-olds before and after they went to a dance. At the dance, sound level meters registered 107 decibels at the center of the dance floor and levels of 120 decibels—more than twice as loud—near the musicians. The research workers found that the average loss of hearing among the young people immediately after the dance was 11½ decibels. (In other words, the intense noise had temporarily raised their hearing thresholds; sounds had to be 11½ decibels *louder* than usual in order to be heard.) One boy

Tests have shown that continued exposure to loud music can cause permanent hearing damage. Musicians who play loud rock music are particularly vulnerable.

suffered a hearing loss of 35 decibels. Several of the young people complained of a ringing in their ears and a kind of muffled feeling. They were also extremely tired.

These tests were designed to measure temporary loss of hearing after a loud noise. However, otologists have found that a ringing in the ears is usually an indication of some permanent injury to the hearing mechanism. Tests made on laboratory animals offer additional evidence that loud music can cause permanent ear damage. Dr. David Lipscomb, of the University of Tennessee at Knoxville, used guinea pigs to study the physical damage caused by continued exposure to the loud noise of rock music played at decibel levels similar to those in dance halls. The left ear of each test animal was plugged to protect it from the noise. The right ear was left unprotected. For three months, the guinea pigs heard loud rock music in four-hour stretches, sometimes every day, sometimes with a day or two off in between. (The schedule was designed to correspond to the random listening patterns of rock fans.)

When the experiment was over, samples of tissue were taken from the animals' inner ears and examined under the microscope. Dr. Lipscomb found that tissue from the left ear, which had been protected by a plug, was normal. Tissue taken from the same area of the unprotected right ear, however, showed serious damage which had reduced the animals' ability to hear. Many of the fine hair cells in the cochlea had become distorted or had collapsed. Some of them were missing altogether. Exposure to the loud music had unquestionably caused permanent injuries to the guinea pigs' hearing.

Because guinea pigs and other laboratory animals have hearing mechanisms similar to man's, experiments like Dr. Lipscomb's provide useful information about noise damage to human hearing. Such laboratory experiments obviously cannot be conducted on human beings themselves, but Dr. Samuel Rosen, the New York ear specialist, has made some field studies of human subjects which have produced startling results. Since 1960, Dr. Rosen has been doing research among the Mabaan people, who live in a remote part of the African Sudan. The Mabaans, who number about 20,000, live in a particularly quiet environment. The loudest noise most of them ever hear occurs during their festivals of singing and dancing, when Mabaan musicians play five-string lyres and beat out rhythms by striking a log with a stick. The normal sound level in a Mabaan village is below 40 decibels, interrupted only by the occasional cry of a rooster, the bleating of a lamb, or the cooing of doves. Mabaans use no guns.

Dr. Rosen found that the hearing of Mabaan people is so acute that they can easily hear each other talking in low conversational tones as far apart as 100 yards. Even more significant, Mabaans lose very little of their hearing as they grow older. An average 75-year-old Mabaan, Dr. Rosen discovered, hears as well as the average American aged 25. His tests also showed that Mabaan people have a particularly good supply of blood to the ears, which helps to keep their hearing acute. The Mabaans' good circulation is partly hereditary, but Dr. Rosen thinks that other factors are also involved. Mabaan diet is low in the saturated fats which cause clogging of the arteries. Moreover, because of the tranquillity of their lives, Mabaan people experience little of the stress from noise which is known to cause constriction and narrowing of the blood vessels.

It seems evident that the Mabaans' peaceful environment not only preserves their hearing but also protects them from other physical damage caused by loud noise. When a sudden noise strikes the human ear, the heart beats rapidly, blood vessels tighten up, and the stomach, esophagus, and intestines contract. German researcher Dr. Gunther Lehmann found that when the small blood vessels constrict in reaction to noise, they become less efficient in carrying their vital blood supplies to the cells of the body. Noise also raises blood pressure and causes the muscles to become tense. Dr. Christiaan Barnard, the South African heart surgeon, has noted that low levels of noise are helpful in the recuperation of heart patients. Therefore he arranged for the telephone to be removed

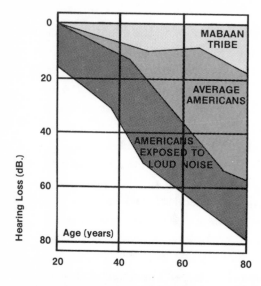

Hearing Loss (dB.)

0 — MABAAN TRIBE

20 — AVERAGE AMERICANS

40 — AMERICANS EXPOSED TO LOUD NOISE

60

80 — Age (years)

20   40   60   80

This graph (left) shows the startling difference between the hearing of Mabaan tribesmen and the hearing of most Americans. The Mabaans, who live in isolated villages in the African Sudan (below), lose much less hearing with age than do the inhabitants of noisier parts of the world.

from the home where his heart transplant patient Philip Blaiberg was recuperating.

Noise affects the digestive system, reducing the flow of saliva and of gastric juices. This reaction often causes nervous indigestion, which can lead to stomach ulcers if the stress from noise continues. Other balances within the body affected by noise include the delicate relationship of water and salt to the hormone produced by the thyroid gland. A disturbance of this balance can cause hypertension and emotional upsets.

Researchers have made tests on laboratory animals which provide additional information about the physical damage noise can do to living things. In one experiment, rats were exposed to the intense noise of a siren; the noise damaged the animals' thymus glands, overstimulated the adrenal glands, and led to gastric ulcers. Tests done at the medical school of the University of California at Los Angeles showed that noise made mice more susceptible to virus infections. Experiments carried out separately in Australia and Argentina indicated that noise interfered with the test animals' kidney functions and caused changes in their hormones. In another test, some rats and rabbits were exposed to continuous loud noise and then compared to a control group of rats and rabbits which had not heard the noise. The animals exposed to the noise developed clogged blood vessels and had heart attacks and strokes. Autopsies showed that physical damage to the heart was much greater than in the control group. The animals' body chemistry had also been changed, and some organs had shrunk.

Other experiments have been carried out which suggest that noise may also be related to allergies, enuresis (involuntary discharge of urine), spinal meningitis, excessive cholesterol in the arteries, loss of equilibrium, and impaired vision. Summing up the physical effects of noise on living things, Dr. Vern O. Knudsen, a leading authority on noise pollution, says: "Noise, like smog, is a slow agent of death."

One of the most frightening things about noise is that we have so little defense against it. When we fall asleep, our closed eyelids protect our eyes from being disturbed by light. But the ears have no such protection. They cannot close, and so they continue to receive the sounds of our environment even while we are asleep. Sometimes the brain learns to tune out continuous and familiar noise. But Dr. Gerd Jansen, working in Germany, has found that even slight noise affects our bodies during sleep; he believes that all sounds which can be heard influence the quality of sleep.

Other researchers have made tests which support Dr. Jansen's findings. Dr. H. R. Richter of Basel, Switzerland, measured the brain waves of sleeping people. He found that noise from vehicles, railroads, jet aircraft, birds, and many other sources often disturbs people's rest even when they are not aware that the quality of their sleep has been damaged. Even relatively quiet noises affect sleep, lifting it from deep, restorative sleep to shallower and less restful levels. Professor Silvan S. Tomkins, formerly of Princeton University, points out: "Anything which disturbs the requisite number of hours of sleep indirectly increases fatigue and pain, and therefore distress." Researchers at Duke University found that women are three times more likely than men to be roused from sleep by noise. They believe this fact may also explain why women suffer from depressive illness twice as often as men—interrupted sleep is known to be related to this kind of illness.

Noise also seems to be a factor in other kinds of mental and emotional illnesses, not only as a result of its physical effects on the body but also because of its direct influence on our thoughts and feelings.

Our reaction to every noise we hear is affected by our total lifetime experience as well as by a complex set of instinctive reactions which have been implanted in us through generations of evolution. The psychologist Sigmund Freud believed that noise can create an anxiety neurosis (an abnormal sense of apprehension) because of the inborn connection between sound and fear. The body instinctively responds to unexpected noise by producing a surge of adrenalin, which gets us ready to react with fear and to flee. Clinical evidence has proved that a startling noise dilates the pupils of the eyes, increases the rate of the heartbeat, and constricts the arteries. These are also reactions of fear.

The way in which noise affects an individual depends largely on what it means to him. However, the most annoying noises are generally those which are unexpected, intermittent, or irregular, those which are high pitched and loud, and come from an unknown source, and those which we do not understand.

The stress of a startling noise is increased if we are already suffering from high levels of background noise. Studies on human beings and on animals have proved that a noise louder than 100 decibels has a startling effect when heard in a quiet environment. But when heard against a background noise of 70 decibels, the same

100-decibel noise will set off much more violent reactions. For instance, heard against the high noise levels of a busy city, sudden loud noises—sirens wailing, children shouting, radios blaring—can cause people to react with violence. Similarly, a man who has worked all day in noisy surroundings may over-react to the noise of a crying baby or a loud television set, even when he has returned to the sanctuary of his quiet home.

Noise is annoying when it seems to be an invasion of privacy or when it distracts us from something we are trying to concentrate on. Background music in an office or elevator is annoying to a person who is trying to work

Noise can prove distracting when people are trying to concentrate on their jobs.

out an idea, yet it does not disturb someone who is thinking about nothing in particular. Conflict between two or more sounds which demand attention from the brain at the same time causes annoyance, confusion, and fatigue. Routine work requiring little concentration is less affected by noise than is exacting work. It has been found that noise, especially at high frequencies, can actually increase the number of errors made in work by causing too high a level of nervous stimulation. Intermittent noise is particularly irritating. Studies show that people never get used to such noise, and that annoyance and disturbing effects increase as the interruptions continue.

Of course, all environmental sound is not necessarily disturbing. Carefully controlled background music can have a soothing effect on people who spend their days doing routine work which may in itself be a little boring. Certain kinds of music can also have a healing effect and are used as therapy in mental hospitals.

But the noise pollution of our daily lives is basically destructive. A series of tests conducted by Dr. Gerd Jansen clearly illustrates this point. Dr. Jansen tested 1,000 workers in 16 steel factories located in Germany's industrial Ruhr valley. Over a period of two years he compared two matched groups of men: one group worked in noise levels over 90 decibels, the other in levels below 90 decibels. The results of the tests showed that workers from the noisier environment were more aggressive and distrustful. More of them showed signs of paranoia, a mental disorder characterized by feelings of persecution. They were more likely to quarrel with their foremen on the job, and twice as many of them had family problems than the men working in the quieter environment.

The stress of working in a noisy environment like this foundry can affect a person's mental and emotional health.

Excessive noise is undoubtedly a factor in many of the mental and emotional problems of modern society. John Handley, an authority on industrial acoustics, says: "Symptoms of hypertension, vertigo, hallucinations, paranoia, and, on occasion, suicidal and homicidal impulses, have been blamed on excessive noise. . . . Noise pollution may be one of the reasons why the incidence of heart disease and mental illness is so high in the United States."

Humans are not, of course, the only victims of noise pollution in the modern world. Most of us have seen animals react with hysterical fear when startled by a loud noise. The sounding of a Civil Defense siren, for instance, often causes a dog to run wild, barking frantically and dashing off with his tail between his legs. A cat may respond more quietly but just as strongly, slinking away to hide. A squirrel will scamper up a tree for safety, where it will sit and shiver with fright.

Animals respond to startling noise with instinctive reactions of fear in just the same way that humans do. The heartbeat is affected, blood vessels constrict, and the balance of the body chemistry is upset. Many animals have hearing mechanisms similar to our own, which can be temporarily or permanently damaged by noise pollution.

There is scientific evidence, too, that noise affects the behavior patterns of animals. In one experiment, rats lost their ability to function sexually after prolonged exposure to noise. Some became homosexual. Others turned cannibal and ate their young. When the noise was continued, the rats eventually died of heart failure.

The sudden, startling noise of sonic booms from military aircraft is known to have a damaging effect on domestic and wild animals. In one case, the sonic booms caused by tests of supersonic military aircraft so seriously disturbed a dachshund that she gave birth prematurely; her litter died soon after birth. A Minnesota farmer claimed that sonic booms had caused his chickens to panic and suffocate themselves against a wall. (He took his case to court and won damages for his loss.) When nesting birds are exposed to sonic booms, they fly off in terror, dislodging and breaking their eggs.

As we have seen, much of the scientific knowledge about noise damage to human beings has been gathered as a result of experiments made on laboratory animals. These same experiments also indicate just how harmful excessive noise is to animals as well. Modern man, with his technological wonders, is subjecting the creatures of the world to growing amounts of noise pollution against which they have no protection.

Damage to Nonliving Things

Did Joshua's trumpets really bring the walls of Jericho tumbling down? We shall probably never know for sure, but modern acoustical engineers believe that such a feat was perfectly possible. It is now known that solid materials, because of their particular molecular structures, have natural resonance frequencies at which they will vibrate if set in motion by some disturbance. A sound vibrating at the same frequency can cause a solid object to break apart. The repeated pressure of the sound waves works its way in among the molecules, destroying their cohesion and separating them from each other. Vibrations which occur because of natural resonance are known as *sympathetic vibrations*. The damage they cause is *acoustic fatigue*.

The principle of natural resonance is involved when a singer holds a particular note with increasing volume and causes a glass to break. The vibrations given off by the voice at this one frequency set up sympathetic vibrations which disturb the arrangement of the molecules in the glass. The glass tries to duplicate the vibrations reaching it through the air. As the volume of the sound increases, the vibrations become stronger. But because glass as a material has little elasticity, it cannot absorb the increasing vibrations. Eventually it will shatter. In a similar manner, a violin at rest, untouched, will try to duplicate the vibrations of the sound of another violin holding a

The British Comet, a commercial jet aircraft developed after World War II, suffered a series of disastrous crashes which were caused by acoustic fatigue.

single note nearby.

Noise spread out over a broad band of frequencies can also be destructive. At levels a little over 150 decibels, it can cause cracks in metal and then make the cracks grow until the metal falls apart. This kind of acoustic fatigue was responsible for the crash of several of Great Britain's Comet jet aircraft. Thorough research after the accidents produced evidence that the noise of the jet engines had vibrated through the planes' fuselages, causing tiny cracks in the metal. The cracks widened until the force of the pressurized air in the cabins caused the fuselages to explode. Three Comets crashed before the rest were grounded and the source of the trouble was discovered.

Similar problems develop in other situations involving high intensity noise. For instance, nuclear reactors generate enormous heat that must be kept under control by cooling liquids circulated at high pressure. The noise of the circulation sometimes reaches levels of 180 to 200 decibels and has been known to cause cracks in the metal of the piping.

Sonic booms can also cause structural damage. The pressure waves of sonic booms have a triggering ability to break up materials held together under stress. In France, three farm workers were killed when a loft full of barley fell on them; the structure of the loft had been broken up by a sonic boom. During a series of tests of sonic booms carried out by the U. S. Air Force over Oklahoma City, plaster cracked on walls, dishes broke in their cabinets, and whole houses vibrated. In the years 1956 to 1968, the Air Force paid out $1.5 million in compensation for damage caused by sonic booms from military aircraft. (More details about the destructive effect of sonic booms will be given in the following chapter.)

4

The Noisemakers

Domestic Noise

While everyone is asleep, the background noise level in a home—especially one in a quiet suburban or rural location—may be no more than a gentle 45 or 55 decibels. The hum of the refrigerator, the light snoring of a sleeper, or muffled noise from outside the house are the only sounds that can be heard.

But the ringing of the alarm clock disturbs this quiet and raises the sound level to a noisy 80 decibels. A baby screaming in the same room produces 92 decibels. Sounds of water running, people talking, a blender whirring in the kitchen, doors slamming, and feet pounding destroy the peaceful quietness. As the day wears on, our homes reverberate with the noise of vacuum cleaners, dishwashers, waste disposals, washing machines and dryers, telephones

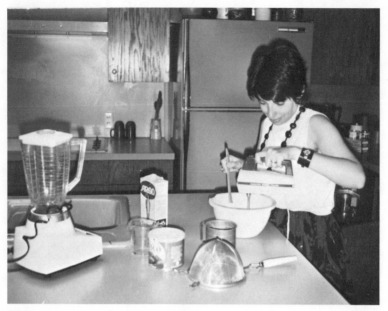

The equipment of a modern kitchen usually includes various kinds of appliances that make food preparation easier and quicker. However, many of these labor-saving devices—mixers, blenders, dishwashers, waste disposals—also contribute to high levels of noise within the home.

and doorbells, radios, televisions, stereos, heating systems, refrigerators, fans, air conditioners, and perhaps one of the new trash compactors, which make a dreadful howling sound.

Most of these pieces of noisy equipment are optional to the basic needs of our lives. We choose to have them because they are convenient, because they lessen the hardship of work and help us get jobs done faster, or because they add to our health, our comfort, or our enjoyment. We choose them because the benefits they offer mean more to us than the nuisance of the noise they cause.

In fact, the noise is not always considered a nuisance, at least not by all listeners. Radios, television sets, and hi-fi equipment are chosen for their ability to make what are welcome sounds to one member of the family, even though they may be unwanted noises to another.

Alone in our own homes, each of us is free to make whatever noise he likes. When other people are present, we have to compromise in order to accommodate a variety of likes and dislikes. If the walls of our dwellings are thin, we must be concerned about the noise we are inflicting on our neighbors. But if we humans are to live up to our reputation as the most intelligent species of life on earth, then we need to be aware of the damage that noise within the home is doing to our own physical and emotional well-being and to that of the people we love.

In the previous chapter we looked at some of the different ways in which noise injures people. Psychiatrist Jack Westman of the University of Wisconsin Medical School believes that the damage caused by noise within the home may be pushing up the divorce rate, widening the generation gap, and breaking down American family life. Dr. Westman feels that most people are unaware of the impact of domestic noises: "We do not realize they are affecting us. We do not understand why we are less effective, less efficient, and more tense. We . . . take out our tensions in other ways. Mothers yell at the youngsters and parents bicker and fight between themselves." Dr. Westman sees noise as one of the chief causes of the "tired mother syndrome," an ailment which "exhibits the same symptoms as combat fatigue; the mother is worn-out, irritable, depressed, tense, and experiences headaches and upset stomachs."

In this expert's opinion, domestic noise has become a serious problem in modern life. Yet although increasing wealth and technology bring more noise into our homes than ever before, they also provide more ways than ever before to control the noise we hear. We can, of course, cover our ears—with waxed ear plugs or with earmuffs. Perhaps if our world continues to grow noisier, we shall wear ear protectors often, just as we now wear sunglasses.

We can listen to radio and television through earphones so that other people are not disturbed by the noise. We can enjoy hi-fi stereo sound of fine quality through headsets, without blasting other members of the family out of the house. Or we can listen to music in an acoustic chair which is wired for sound and egg-shaped to keep the sound from spreading out into the room. We can listen through a flat disc held against the ear, a device like those often used in hospitals.

When buying a piece of machinery for the home, we can consider the amount of noise it makes as a reason for choosing one model rather than another. Too often we seem to choose unnecessarily noisy household equipment. Ray Donley, chief engineer of Hearing Conservation Incorporated in Detroit, believes that most people expect a vacuum cleaner, for instance, to make a loud noise as proof of its powerful cleaning action. Equipment *can* be manufactured to operate quietly—by using precision engineering, by packing the gears of the motor in grease, and by building the casing of sound-absorbing materials. But this costs extra money. So far, consumer demand for quiet appliances is only just beginning to be strong enough to persuade manufacturers that the more expensive quiet models are worth producing.

An acoustic chair provides a means of listening to music without disturbing others or being disturbed by domestic noises. The egg-shaped chair encloses the listener in an environment of sound but prevents the sound waves from spreading out into the room.

Quieter garbage cans, however, are proving popular despite their extra cost. For a long time city laws, made for the sake of hygiene, specified that garbage cans had to be all steel, which made them, of course, very noisy to use. But gradually many of these laws are being changed so that cans of quiet heavy plastic or rubber can be used. Bethlehem Steel is making a steel garbage can in which the clang has been replaced with a thud by the addition of a sound-absorbing underseal, an asphalt belt, and rubber feet. New York City has introduced garbage bags which are hygienic and quiet. They are also made of biodegradable material which eventually breaks down into natural components in a way that plastics will not. Thus the bags can be disposed of in sanitary landfills.

Besides protecting our ears from noise and controlling the amount of noise we make at home, we can also build

Bethlehem Steel's new garbage can (left) is much less noisy than the conventional model (right). It has a sound-absorbing undercoat and six rubber feet which cushion shocks. Strips of asphalt felt around the can and on the lid also help to dampen vibrations.

and furnish our homes so that noise will be absorbed and deadened. A wall can be made soundproof by building it so that each side vibrates independently of the other. In this way, the noise is not conducted through the wall as it is when both sides are fixed to the same studs and vibrate in unison, like a drum. Cinderblocks used within a wall also deaden sound by providing a honeycomb of tiny dead-air spaces. So does soft and fluffy insulation material or plastic foam, which are also effective as heat insulation. At points in the wall where these materials are not used—for instance, around electrical outlets, medicine cabinets, or plumbing outlets placed back to back—noise will be carried through to the other side. However, plumbing can be made quieter by inserting cork or other insulating material around the piping wherever it comes in contact with the structure of the house.

New York is the first city in the United States to write provisions protecting people against noise into its building codes. New residential buildings in the city must now be built with sufficient noise insulation to cut the penetration of noise by 45 decibels. In buildings which go up after 1972, noise penetration must be cut still further, by 50 decibels. These provisions were adopted largely as a result of campaigning by a dedicated antinoise organization, Citizens for a Quieter City.

The furnishings we choose can also help to cut down noise in the home. Carpets, draperies, and upholstered furniture all reduce the reverberations of noise bouncing to and fro between walls, floor, and ceiling. Carpets deaden the sound of footsteps. Heavy drapes can absorb outside noise as it comes in through window glass. Acoustic panels of cork or polystyrene foam also deaden noise by

Sound-absorbing materials like this perforated ceramic tile can be used to lower noise levels in homes and offices.

preventing the sound waves from bouncing about.

By using these soundproofing techniques, we can reduce the noise in our homes and help to keep every member of the family healthier and happier. The same methods also help to keep the noise we make confined within our own homes so that it does not annoy our neighbors.

Neighborhood Noise

Within our own homes the noise we make is very much our own affair. But once we move outside, it becomes of concern to the whole neighborhood. And, of course, the noise that other people make outside their homes concerns us as well.

Some of us dislike noise. Others enjoy it. However, the list of noises that one individual enjoys is likely to be very different from the list of noises that anyone else enjoys. The kids who race around the block on tricycles with noisemakers flipping across the spokes of the wheels, or with wind sirens howling, are not bothered by their own noise. They love it. It makes them feel powerful, makes them feel that they are riding faster. The neighbor nursing a toothache hates the noise—maybe he would hate it even if he were feeling perfectly fit. Certainly not many people are fond of the noises of power lawn mowers, leaf rakers, chain saws, snow blowers, snowmobiles, and trail bikes which destroy the tranquillity of many suburban neighborhoods.

Many of our most valuable public servants are vigorous noisemakers. The police, the fire department, the sanitation department, all bring unwanted noise into our neighborhoods along with the essential community services they provide. As traffic noise rises higher and higher, the sirens of police cars, ambulances, and fire trucks are being designed to make louder and louder noises. Many cities place no controls on these devices and never test them. Rarely do the authorities insist that sirens beam their noise ahead only, in the direction that the vehicle is traveling. Civil Defense sirens in some areas are tested every week, despite the protests of people who live nearby. Sanitation departments are rarely given the extra money they need to buy modern, quiet trucks for garbage collection.

In the category of community noisemakers, there are some quaint holdovers from earlier days, particularly in company towns where one industry dominates the economy of the area. The whole town of Lead, South Dakota, for instance, wakes up at six o'clock each morning to the shrill of the 15-horse-power whistle blown by the Homestake Mining Company. Lead is located in a quiet valley, with its homes climbing up the surrounding hillsides. The noise of the whistle, trapped in the valley, reverberates between the hills, especially on days when clouds hang low and hold the sound in. At seven o'clock the whistle blows again, and then at intervals throughout the day, indicating meal breaks and changes of shift. For years it has also blown at nine each evening as a warning that children should be off the streets.

Lead's noise problem is unusual, but many other communities are fighting their own battles against noise. The United States has, so far, no national noise abatement laws controlling levels of noise to be heard around neighborhoods. What laws there are have been set at the state and city level, most of them in the form of nuisance ordinances, which are very difficult to enforce. Many of the local ordinances relating to noise apply at nighttime only. Memphis, however, is one of the few cities in the nation which takes pride in eliminating noise. It calls itself the Quiet City and has strong noise ordinances which are stringently enforced. Each year a thousand horn-honkers are charged in Memphis. The city awards prizes to its school children for essays against noise and honors its "Silent Citizens" who muffle their power mowers.

There are various methods which can be used to control neighborhood noise. Zoning can help, for example, by preventing trucks from driving through a residential district. Some communities deliberately turn their residential thoroughfares into a maze of one-way streets to discourage through traffic and heavy trucks from using them. Housing developers can use dead-end streets to limit the volume of traffic. Houses and apartment complexes can be set at angles which allow a minimum of noise to bounce up from the roadway or from the neighbors' backyards. They can also be screened from noise by trees and bushes.

The latest census figures show that Americans continue to move from the country into the cities and metropolitan areas. Most of us like to be near jobs, hospitals, stores, theaters, firehouses, banks, schools, and other centers of community life. But we suffer when the accumulated noise of city life ends up in our own backyard.

Traffic Noise

Of all the forms of noise pollution which add to the stress of life in metropolitan areas, noise from traffic is the most persistent. Cars, motor bikes, trucks, and buses give off noise from their engines, exhaust pipes, tires, horns, and from the air turbulence around their bodywork as they move at high speed. These noises bounce off the hard pavement and are reflected to and fro between buildings. Wherever people are trying to concentrate on reading, writing, talking, listening, sleeping, or any other everyday activity, some parts of their brains are being distracted by the noise of traffic.

In the United States, cities and suburbs were designed for car owners, high priority being given to the convenience offered by freeways, highways, wide roads, and parking lots. Since land was plentiful, communities spread out widely, so that often a car was necessary to get to school, to work, and to the store. Because people found it so convenient to use cars, there was little demand for public transport. But gradually our dearly beloved automobiles, with all their emotional appeals of power, freedom, and status, have come to be seen as the monsters which may strangle our society. Their numbers increase even faster than the population, and more and more land has to be paved over for roads in order to avoid traffic jams. Their exhaust fumes cause dangerous air pollution. The noise they make threatens our health and sanity.

There are well over 100 million motor vehicles in the United States, more than half the number of vehicles in the world. They are grinding to a standstill in the cities, speeding their way across the wide open spaces of the country. Of these 100 million, nearly 90 million are automobiles, each making a noise somewhere between 65 and 85 decibels, with the average falling at about 76 decibels. Each of the 16.5 million trucks and 1.5 million buses makes a much louder noise, often 95 decibels and even more. The 2.4 million motorcycles in the United States are noisy beasts too, often reaching sound levels of 110 and 120 decibels.

The "quiet" family car is the most familiar and most numerous of the automotive noisemakers. Since its noise-producing parts are typical of those of other vehicles, we will look at them in detail.

Motor vehicles crowd the streets of the nation's cities, polluting the environment with exhaust fumes and loud noise.

Most cars are driven by an internal combustion engine that burns gasoline to produce power by means of a continuing series of explosions in the cylinders. The gases produced by these explosions are released from the engine through the exhaust pipe. But because the exhaust gases are hot and under pressure, they make a loud noise if they are released directly into the cooler outside air. The muffler on the exhaust pipe is designed to reduce this noise; it allows the gases to expand and cool by diffusing them through a series of baffles. But the toxic gases in the exhaust react with the metal of the muffler, gradually destroying it. As the metal wears away, the muffler is

53

An automobile muffler that has been damaged by corrosive gases is less efficient in reducing noise from the exhaust.

less able to deaden noise. When the muffler falls off altogether, the noise from the engine exhaust is deafening.

Some people seem to believe that excessive noise from their car exhaust gives them a sporty, dashing style which impresses others. As a result, some sports cars are fitted with mufflers which are specially made to preserve the noise of the exhaust by letting the explosive sounds through and even amplifying them with resonators. The noise produced by this kind of sports car reaches 90 decibels or more, well above the level which is known to cause damage to hearing over a period of time.

The energy produced by the gasoline exploding in the cylinders is transmitted to the wheels of the car through moving metal parts, most of which make some kind of noise as they turn and rub against each other. As in the manufacture of domestic appliances, some of this noise can be reduced by using high-grade metal and making the engine to precise measurements, by packing the gears well in grease, and by building a heavy casing around the motor to contain the noise. But all these improvements cost money, and for years most manufacturers and most consumers considered them an unnecessary expense, a luxury just for the wealthy few. Gradually, however, attitudes are changing. Now the makers of some popular medium-price cars advertise built-in quietness as a positive selling point.

Noise is also produced by air turbulence around the bodywork of a moving car. Every blunt projection from the car's body causes wind noise because it interferes with the smooth flow of air over the car as it moves forward. Wind noises also resonate in hollows of the body which are not shaped aerodynamically—that is, in accordance with the principles of air movement around objects. Narrow crevices or badly fitting windows cause the wind to scream. The noise of air turbulence can be greatly reduced by shaping the bodywork of the car in a "clean" aerodynamic design. Today skillful automobile designers are gradually learning more about using the principles of clean aerodynamics to make quieter cars.

Tires are another continuous source of noise, especially when a car is traveling at high speeds. They vibrate on contact with the road, and their vibrations are transmitted through the wheels and the axles into the body so that the whole car vibrates and causes still more noise. Some of the noise which starts with the tires can be deadened by rubber suspension systems, rubber body mounts, and sound-absorbing materials used in floor-

When a vehicle is moving at high speeds, its tires make a continuous noise as they come in contact with the pavement.

boards, carpets, door panels, and interior roofing.

But some of the noise produced by the tires is unavoidable. Basically tires are designed for safety—to grip the road and give positive steering and good control when braking. To this end they have grooves cut in the treads, which set up a constant noise as they slap against the roadway. Snow tires, with extra deep grooves and sometimes with studs, make even more noise than regular tires when driven on a clear road. No technology exists yet to make tires which are safe and also silent. All we can do at the moment is to stop tire noise from spreading unnecessarily through the car.

The horn is the one part of an automobile which is purposely designed to make a noise; it is required by law to be ready for use to avoid accidents. If this were literally the only time horns were used, few of us would complain. But too often they are used to express anger and impatience with other drivers, to attract the attention of a friend on the street, or to say good-bye as we leave a party. Most automobile horns today produce a noise of about 90 decibels, but they are regularly being made louder so that they can be heard against the rising levels of noise in city traffic. Not surprisingly, a friendly toot of 90 decibels has the unfriendly result of upsetting a lot of people.

Much of the noise made by our automobile is left behind in the environment as we drive along. But some of it travels with us, resounding through the vehicle. In addition, there is the noise caused by heaters, air conditioners, radios, stereo tape players, and reverberators. As we have seen, noise distracts the brain when it is trying to concentrate on something else, causing fatigue and stress. Thus, noise inside the car becomes a contributing factor in traffic accidents and in family quarrels on long journeys.

Motorcycles are well known for the noise they make. Their tires, however, produce less noise than those of automobiles; after all, they have only two. Most cycles also cause less air turbulence noise, even though they are not aerodynamically clean, because they have less bulk than an automobile. The noise from exhaust and engine, however, is very much louder than that from an automobile. The engine of a motorcycle is fully exposed, so that the noise coming from the cylinders is not deadened by a heavy casing. Because the powerful noise of motor bikes is one of their strong selling features, they are often deliberately fitted with ineffective mufflers. Sometimes the owner takes off the muffler altogether or replaces it with one which is purposely designed to be noisy, despite

Because the engine of a motorcycle is not surrounded by a heavy casing, the noise it makes goes directly into the environment.

the fact that this violates many vehicle codes as well as local noise ordinances. Hawaii is one of the few states which makes it specifically unlawful to ride a motorcycle fitted with a muffler designed to increase noise.

Trucks and buses make extra loud noises because their noisemaking parts are larger and more numerous than those of the average family car. They have bigger engines, often with casings made of metal which is too thin to do a good job of containing the noise. They often have inadequate mufflers. Most of them have a massive bulk, clumsily designed, which causes a lot of noisy air turbulence. They have enormous tires, frequently in large numbers, with very deep grooves to make sure that they hold the road. At low speeds it is the engine transmission of trucks and buses which makes the most noise. At high speeds the tires, the exhaust, and air turbulence are the chief culprits. As trucks and buses get older, they tend to get noisier. The vibrations of their massive engines shake loose the seals around the engine compartments, the metal becomes distorted, and more noise escapes.

The Department of Transportation's Urban Mass Transportation Administration has designed Environmental Improvement Kits to reduce noise and air pollution from buses. The kits make use of improved mufflers and special engine mountings which reduce noise transmission. They are being tested in Washington, D.C., San Antonio, and San Francisco. If they prove effective, we can look forward to quieter and cleaner bus routes.

So far, the various vehicles used for mass transit—buses, trains, subway cars—each make more noise individually than the automobile. But because they can move thousands of people at a time, their total noise is very much less. On one lane of an expressway, 4,500 cars can move past one point in an hour; in the same length of time, 70,000 people can be moved over one rail track. However, at present any one person traveling by car will have a quieter journey than if he travels by train, subway, or bus. Perhaps as we learn to care about our mass transit systems, we shall be able to develop ways of making them run more quietly.

We can also do much more than we do now to design and build roadways so that their noise causes less blight on the surroundings. A road which runs in a cutting, below ground level, contains its own noise. By the time the noise of the vehicles reaches up to the surface, much of

This air vent is part of an improved exhaust system included in the Environmental Improvement Kit for buses. The kits are used to modify existing buses so that they produce less noise and air pollution.

it has faded away. Ground-level roads are noisier, but they are also cheaper to build. Trees and bushes can be planted around ground-level highways to reduce noise by dispersing it among their leaves and branches. Elevated roadways are the noisiest kind of all, because they spray their noise around in every direction without effective baffles.

The states of New York and California have laws fixing maximum decibel levels for various kinds of vehicles using the public highways. But the job of enforcing these laws is so expensive and time-consuming that it is not often carried out effectively. New York state troopers with hand-held sound level meters are sometimes stationed at tollbooths along some of the state's expressways. The entire California Highway Patrol has only three noise level meters. Yet in Stockholm, Sweden, most policemen carry noise level meters, and have and use the power to give tickets on the spot for violations of the noise laws. American communities will have to follow Stockholm's example if traffic noise in the United States is to be brought under control.

Aircraft Noise

Airplanes have become our most popular form of mass transit, accounting for two-thirds of the total passenger miles traveled in the United States by all mass transit systems put together. When an airplane reaches a cruising height of 30,000 feet or more on a long flight, it can scarcely be heard from the ground. But on shorter flights at lower altitudes, and during take-off and landing, the noise produced by planes is maddening. A study carried out on people living close to London's Heathrow Airport showed that many more of them suffered from mental

Every time a jet plane comes in to land or takes off, people living close to the airport are disturbed by the noise of its engines.

illness serious enough to require treatment than a similar group of people living in a quieter area some distance away from the airport.

O'Hare Airport in Chicago has the reputation of being the busiest airport in the world. It averages 2,100 flights a day; at peak times, an aircraft takes off or lands every 30 seconds. In 1965, the Federal Aviation Administration (FAA) estimated that noise from O'Hare affected 235,000 people in a 72-square-mile area. By 1975, the noise pollution will reach even farther, extending over an area of 123 square miles and affecting 432,000 people. A total of 86 schools were affected by noise from O'Hare in 1965. By 1975, classes in 142 schools will be disturbed by the noise of the jets. Unless schools around O'Hare and other airports can add efficient soundproofing to their buildings, the education of millions of young people will suffer. One estimate made in the Los Angeles area showed that 50,000 students lose up to three hours of study time a day because of the noise from jet aircraft using the Los Angeles airport.

In the United States today, there are 564 airports which are used by scheduled airlines, and an additional 7,000 used by military and private aircraft. The fight to cut down noise near these airports is being waged on three major fronts.

One way to reduce noise is to develop quieter aircraft, and one of the most effective ways to encourage such development is strict regulation of maximum noise levels. The Federal Aviation Administration has the job of fixing noise limits on all new aircraft. Right now, big jets make noises over 105 decibels within four miles of the start of their take-off run. The FAA hopes to cut this down to a maximum of 95 decibels—still a damaging level of noise but less than half as loud as the present 105 dBs.

Kennedy Airport in New York has set its own noise limits for jets on take-off, and it monitors each departure with sound level meters placed beyond the end of the runway. Airlines operating planes which exceed the noise limits are fined. To keep their fines down, the airlines have gotten together and set up their own noise monitoring units at the end of the runway. Operators warn the pilots by radio when their noise levels are rising too high and should be reduced. Signs beside the runways at many major airports now remind pilots to "observe noise abatement procedures."

Faced with the increasing number of noise regulations, the aircraft industry has begun to develop quieter planes. The Boeing 747 "jumbo" jet, when operated for minimum noise, can now keep within the FAA's proposed 95-decibel limit on take-off. Lockheed has developed a sound-absorbing material which can be used to line the ducts of jet aircraft engines. The material contains honeycombed metal pockets which trap noise and dissipate it in the form of heat. As noise regulations become stricter, manufacturers will no doubt discover other methods of making quieter planes.

A second way in which the nuisance of airplane noise can be reduced is by controlling land development around new airports. A Federal Aviation Administration official

This man is using a sound level meter to measure the noise made by a jet on take-off. Some airports are trying to reduce airplane noise by setting noise regulations and enforcing them.

has suggested that new regional airports should be built on 40-square-mile plots which include a 24-square-mile noise cushion of land that could be used for farming, recreation, and open space but not for homes, schools, or businesses.

This suggestion makes sense, but unfortunately it is not always easy to put into action. There are deep conflicts between the advantages of a conveniently located airport and the blight of noise and air pollution which it causes. Most major cities want their airports as close to the downtown area as possible for the convenience of business travelers who help to increase the prosperity of the area. Some property owners want new airports located close to their own holdings because the commerce that usually springs up around airports is likely to push up the value of their property. Other property owners, especially those who own homes, want the airport as far away as possible to avoid the noise.

When airports are located near residential neighborhoods, drastic measures are sometimes necessary to solve the noise problems that arise. For many years, people living near Los Angeles International Airport suffered from ever-increasing noise as jet planes got bigger and flights became more frequent. In 1970, a new runway was opened which brought the intense noise of landing and take-off even closer to home for people in the Westchester area. Angry crowds mobbed the meetings of the airport commissioners, protesting the noise. Finally an agreement was hammered out; the airport commission and the city of Los Angeles would buy from their owners the houses most severely affected by the noise. The prices to be paid for individual homes ranged between $28,000 and $115,000, and the total cost of the project added up to about $300 million. The houses purchased would either be torn down or resold at low prices to contractors who were prepared to move them elsewhere. In 1972, when the project is completed, 75 square blocks which once were home to 8,000 people will be deserted. Noise from the airport will no longer disturb the neighborhood because there will be no one there to hear it.

Even when an airport is built far away from residential areas, problems can still arise. In New Orleans, the new international airport was built a good 20 miles out of town to protect citizens from pollution. But no zoning laws covered the areas along the road leading from the airport to the city. The real estate people moved in, and housing developments went up rapidly. A residential area now exists close to the airport despite the good intentions of the original planners.

There is a third method of reducing airplane noise which can make life pleasanter for people living near existing airports. It involves altering flight patterns and techniques so that the noise is directed away from densely populated areas. Noise can be reduced by bringing aircraft in on a steep angle of approach and by having them take off under reduced power, while still leaving a wide margin for safety. Flight paths can be directed over rivers, lakes, bays, and railroads. Night flights can be forbidden without special permission. (Permission might reasonably be given when, for instance, an aircraft has passed through several time zones during a long flight and arrival during regular operating hours becomes impossible.) "Stacking" of aircraft can be carried out in ways which minimize noise. At busy airports, arriving planes some-

Airport workers wear ear protectors to shield themselves from the high levels of noise on the airfield.

times have to "stack up" to await their turn to land. The control tower acknowledges their arrival and gives them instructions to circle at a particular altitude, from which they gradually drop down until it is their turn to land. These stacks can be located over sparsely populated areas and held at heights which cause little annoyance at ground level until the final OK for landing is given.

Helicopters are capable of making even more noise than some of the big jets: a large helicopter can be four times as noisy as a jet plane. Because they need only a small landing area, helicopters can land and take off right in the center of heavily populated cities. This makes them a particular noise hazard. A regular helicopter service to New York airports from the Pan Am building in Manhattan was stopped because the noise reverberated intolerably through the streets bordered by tall buildings. An alternative plan has been proposed which would allow the helicopters to land on a pier projecting into the East River and would confine the part of the flight close to New York City to the area over the river.

During the Vietnam war, a new, quiet helicopter was developed for military use; a helicopter which could sneak in quietly over the jungle treetops stood much less chance of being shot down than a noisy chopper. In this case the incentive was strong enough to get a quiet machine developed. If we fight fiercely enough for strict noise abatement laws in our home towns, then there will be strong incentives to develop quiet machines for peaceful uses too.

In 1971, the United States Congress voted down the further development of the supersonic transport plane, generally referred to as the SST. This plane, flying faster than the speed of sound, would have crisscrossed continents and oceans, laying down carpets of sonic booms capable of doing enormous damage to people, to animals, annd to material things. Military aircraft have been flying at supersonic speeds for many years and have already provided plenty of well-documented evidence of damage done by sonic booms.

In August 1966, a sonic boom dislodged 80 tons of rock which fell onto prehistoric Indian cliff dwellings in Arizona's Canyon de Chelly National Monument and partially destroyed them. In Bryce Canyon, Utah, a sonic boom caused sandstone columns to crumble and fall on Indian relics. Such damage does not necessarily happen all at

A plane moving at supersonic speeds creates a cone-shaped shock wave which trails behind it. The sonic boom carpet is formed where the cone intersects with the ground.

once. One boom may cause a slight disintegration, then later booms cause the structure to fall. In the high Alps sonic booms have triggered off avalanches. When a sonic boom struck a mink farm in Minnesota, the female mink leaped from their nesting boxes. Later, dead mink were found in the cages, some of them partially eaten. In Switzerland a sonic boom caused a prime herd of cattle to stampede over a cliff.

Some of the clearest evidence of sonic boom damage comes from a series of boom tests conducted by the United States Air Force from 1961 to 1967. The many claims which the Air Force has had to pay as a result of these tests indicate that sonic booms are a dangerous and destructive addition to the other dangerous noises produced by aircraft.

Damage Payments Resulting from Air Force Sonic Boom Tests

City	Population	Approximate Number of Booms	Complaints	Claims Filed	Claims Paid	Amount Paid
Oklahoma City (1964)	324,253	1,252	15,452	4,901	289	$123,061
Chicago (1965)	3,550,404	49	7,128	3,156	1,464	116,229
St. Louis (1961-62)	750,026	151	5,000	1,624	825	58,648
St. Louis (1965)	750,026	23	1,390	491	215	17,036
Milwaukee (1965)	741,324	61	953	639	259	12,652
Pittsburgh (1965)	604,332	50	1,848	1,102	503	30,808
Edwards AFB (1966-67)	45,000	37	62	19	16	1,399

Construction Noise

"What goes up must come down" might well be the motto of the construction industry in the United States today. Within our cities hundreds of buildings, some still in good condition, are being torn down and replaced with new buildings. In addition, important urban renewal projects are replacing inadequate slum housing with new homes which offer more humane living conditions. In city and countryside alike, giant earth-moving equipment alters the face of the earth as it gouges out new highways. The machines used in the construction business are enormously powerful—and hideously noisy.

Every day in American cities, old buildings are being torn down and new buildings constructed in their place. Noise is an inevitable by-product of both operations.

Heavy earth-moving machines, such as big bulldozers, operate at noise levels of 100 decibels or more, a great deal higher than the 85-decibel level which is known to cause permanent hearing loss when experienced for five or more hours a day. A jackhammer, when heard from 50 feet away, makes a noise measuring 85 decibels; at the source the noise measures 110 dBs. An excavating machine makes a noise of 110 decibels; an air hammer, 115 dBs; a riveter, 115 dBs. All these machines, and many more, are often working at the same time on the same construction site. Their combined noise deafens the construction workers and drives people living and working near the site to distraction.

Each year the inhabitants of New York City are bombarded by noise from 100,000 building and demolition projects and 80,000 street repair projects. This unrelenting noise drove Robert Alex Baron to found Citizens for a Quieter City, an organization of business and professional leaders dedicated to fighting noise pollution in New York. Citizens for a Quieter City has been pressuring the mayor and the city council for stricter noise control laws. The organization also informs the general public about the dangers of noise and acts as a clearing house for information about developments of quieter construction machinery in various parts of the world.

So far no one has had much success in reducing the noise from some of the biggest machines, although the noise they make can to some extent be contained within the construction area by screening it off. Smaller pieces of equipment such as jackhammers, however, can be quieted down considerably by fitting them with fiber-filled mufflers which shroud the length of the machine. At first,

Con Edison's cookie cutter lifts a concrete "cookie" from the pavement. The new machine can cut holes in concrete with one-third the noise of a pneumatic drill.

operators dislike the muffled jackhammer because it is clumsier to operate than an unmuffled one, but they soon learn to use it accurately. Noise from powerful hoisting machines can be contained by placing baffles around the equipment. A new machine developed by Consolidated Edison, the electric power company in New York, cuts out round holes in concrete with only one-third of the noise of a pneumatic drill and in one-third of the time. The machine, familiarly known as the cookie cutter, has a five-inch core which is fed with water lubrication to keep down noise and dust.

Although some silencing techniques for construction equipment now exist and more are gradually being developed, construction companies have had little incentive to invest the money and effort needed to put them to use. Effective noise control laws will be required to force them to do so, and effective laws will be passed and enforced only if citizens make public officials understand that this is what they want.

In New York City, daytime construction, between 7 A.M. and 6 P.M., is exempted from any noise control. Controls exist for nighttime operations, but variances frequently are granted on the grounds that the disturbance is "temporary and necessary." Construction noise could be controlled by officials in purchasing departments of cities and corporations, who could write into their building contracts strict limits on the amount of noise that may be made. If enough people make enough fuss, companies may begin to find that such noise control regulations will help them to keep the goodwill of their buying public.

Construction workers themselves often suffer most from construction noise. They work for eight hours a day or more surrounded by noise levels well over 100 decibels. In one on-site study, all 66 men working on the project were found to have significant changes in their hearing ability, resulting in some degree of permanent deafness. Earmuffs have not yet become compulsory or even normal equipment for construction workers and have met with some opposition from the tough-guy attitudes of workers on building sites. But they can be helpful in protecting hearing and in preventing other physical and mental deterioration caused by the very high levels of noise. There is no reason why construction workers should not wear earmuffs regularly in just the same way that airport workers wear them in the service areas near the ramps.

Industrial Noise

According to figures published by the Surgeon General, more than 6 million workers in the United States—perhaps even as many as 16 million—earn their living under conditions which are dangerous to their hearing. The Public Health Service reports that the number of workers subjected to potentially harmful levels of noise probably exceeds the number exposed to any other significant hazard at work.

Noise at work became a major problem as the industrial revolution developed, and the nation changed from a quiet agricultural economy to a noisy industrial economy. (Today a lot of agricultural work has become noisy too, with the use of heavy tractors, reaping and threshing machines, and many other aids to farmers.) Some of the noisiest of industrial jobs are in machine shops, foundries, stamping mills, and other plants where heavy machinery cuts, welds, pounds, and explodes metal into the many intricate shapes required by our technological society. Cotton mills are also wretchedly noisy places. So are sawmills. In other industries the forced draft of air in chimney stacks, furnaces, compressors, and cooling towers makes a deafening roar. The flow of air blown off from safety valves at high pressure travels at supersonic speeds and is, therefore, very noisy.

Loss of hearing caused by noise on the job is now

A drop hammer is one of the noisy machines used in the metal-working industry. Driven by steam or electric power, the hammer shapes hot metal by pounding it into dies, or molds.

treated as an occupational disease. It has become the duty of the employer to keep noise levels down or to provide ear protectors. If he does not, and his workers suffer hearing loss as a result, then the employer has to pay compensation in amounts related to the degree of hearing lost. Each state sets its own price on compensation of this kind. In Michigan a worker gets compensation of $28,500 for total loss of hearing in both ears. In Nebraska, a worker gets $3,700 for the same damage. In New York he gets $150 a week for 60 weeks—a total of $9,000. In a number of states, a worker must leave his job for several months to prove that his hearing loss is permanent before he can claim compensation. Many workers, naturally, do not want to take this risk and so do not receive the compensation to which they have a right. The Federal Council of Science and Technology has reported that if only 10 percent of workers eligible for hearing loss compensation filed claims and received an average of $1,000 each, then the total compensation could reach $450 million.

Studies have been made of the effects of industrial noise on human hearing. Researchers for the U. S. Public Health Service carried out tests over several years in the workshops of four federal prisons, measuring the noise levels that workers were exposed to and the amount of hearing they lost as a result. In the cotton mill at Atlanta prison the noise level in the weaving department was regularly 103 decibels; in the beaming, twisting, and spinning sections, it was 96 to 97 decibels. The noise in the wood furniture factory at Leavenworth was over 97 decibels, and in the metal factory at Lewisburg prison the noise ran over 100 decibels. The researchers found a universal deterioration of hearing among prisoners working in these factories. Workers in the weaving section of the Atlanta cotton mill suffered the most severe hearing loss.

Other tests made on jute weavers in Dundee, Scotland, also revealed serious hearing loss resulting from industrial noise. The weavers were women who had worked in the plant for an average of 34 years each; half of them had to sit up in front to be able to enjoy public meetings, church services, or movies. Three-fourths of the women disliked or were unable to use the telephone, and two-thirds of them used lip reading or sign language, especially on the job.

As mentioned in Chapter 3, loud noise heard over a long period of time can cause other physical damage in addition to hearing loss. Dr. Gunther Lehmann found that workers in a noisy German boiler factory suffered constantly from damaged blood circulation, which caused destruction of cells in their ears and in other organs of the body.

Thus, a large body of evidence indicates that noise at work robs people of their hearing and causes other physical disorders. The tests on steel workers referred to earlier showed that noise levels over 90 decibels affects emotional stability as well, tending to make workers agressive and paranoid. Noise also can kill, by contributing to industrial accidents. It has been proved that noise above levels of 90 decibels causes a significant increase in errors at work, even among people who are accustomed to noise. And errors made while working with dangerous machinery can easily lead to injury and death. Noise also increases the number of industrial accidents because it hides sounds which might indicate a breakdown in equipment.

In 1968, the Secretary of Labor drew up federal regulations which set a maximum noise level of 85 decibels on the job for industries with government contracts over the value of $10,000. This noise level was fiercely contested by industrialists, and after some hard bargaining a compromise figure of 90 decibels was reached. (Because of the logarithmic nature of the decibel scale, the 90-decibel figure more than doubled the maximum noise level allowed.) The new regulation was then incorporated into an already existing law, the Walsh-Healey Public Contracts Act. But the law's 90-decibel limit did not give workers full protection against excessive noise, since continued exposure to noise louder than 85 decibels is known to damage hearing. And the federal regulations did nothing at all to protect the millions of workers who were not involved in government contract work, or whose companies held only small contracts. However, these same provisions for maximum noise exposure have since been extended to other areas of United States commerce by the

The General Motors foundry at Defiance, Ohio, has been specially designed to incorporate modern noise control techniques. The molding machine shown here is completely enclosed by four-inch-thick acoustical panels, which absorb excess noise.

Occupational Safety and Health Act of 1970, which came into force in April 1971.

Noise levels in factories can be reduced in many different ways. Silencers can be fitted to various pieces of equipment: a series of small baffles can be used to split up a solid roar of noise, or a piece of soft material known as a stack-stuffer can be hung in a chimney stack. Machines can be placed on beds of sound-insulating material which separate them from the floor and prevent vibrations from being transmitted into the structure of the building. Noisy machines can have noise barriers erected around them, or they can be placed in acoustic recesses or compartments.

Some of the established processes within a factory can be replaced by others which are quieter yet equally effective. In some cases, for instance, metal can be joined by quiet compression methods instead of by noisy riveting. Metal makes less noise if it is heated before it is worked. Equipment can be driven by quiet electric motors instead of noisy internal combustion engines.

There are also ways in which workers themselves can be protected against excessive noise. The length of time during which any one worker is exposed to an unavoidably loud noise can be regulated by rotating the noisiest jobs among several people. Ear protectors can be more generally worn. The noise to which a worker is exposed can be measured on a practical and inexpensive instrument known as a noise exposure computer interrogator. This device adds up the noise levels experienced by an individual during the day and can be used to check his total exposure against the federal guidelines for occupational safety.

This machine operator is wearing a noise exposure meter, a device which measures noise levels and records the amount of exposure to excessive noise.

Urged on by the noise regulations of the Walsh-Healey Act and by the principal of legal compensation for hearing loss caused at work, employers are slowly beginning to take more responsibility for reducing the amounts of noise their workers are exposed to. Some progress has been made in protecting workers from noise on the job. But much more action is needed.

Noise for Fun

Most of the noisemakers we have looked at so far produce their noise as an unwelcome by-product of their proper function. We may tolerate such noise but we certainly do not enjoy it. But how much would we enjoy a football game without the roar of appreciative fans? Would a party be fun without the clamor of music and conversation? Is not every person who slips his coin into a jukebox casting his vote *in favor* of noise? Apparently there are many noises, some of them harmfully loud, which we choose to make for fun.

People who go shooting subject their own ears to sudden loud noises of 130 decibels. A study made in Florida on 103 hunters and members of a gun club showed that most of them had suffered some permanent hearing loss, particularly in their left ears. (The butt of the gun pressed against the right shoulder protects the right ear from some of the shock waves of the loud noise.) Because this kind of hearing damage builds up over a period of time, it was found that regular skeet shooters and weapons instructors had been more seriously affected than had occasional hunters.

People who regularly listen to music amplified to 100 or 120 decibels are also indulging in a dangerous form of entertainment. Pop musicians are particularly vulnerable. The New York otologist Dr. Samuel Rosen made tests on a group of musicians who worked for a few hours several days each week at noise levels around 114 decibels. He found their hearing to be much less acute than is normal for young people of their age. Perhaps our pop music idols are paying too high a price for their success.

Many of the people who enjoy these noisy forms of entertainment may not know that they are inflicting on themselves gradual but permanent loss of hearing, plus the possibility of other physical and emotional damage. However, we have plenty of evidence which indicates that, even when they do know, many continue to take their pleasure in the same noisy ways. Some people like to live close to a busy traffic route because the noise and movement prevent them from feeling lonely. Where we live, how we entertain ourselves—these things are matters of personal choice. It would be sad if we made the choice without knowledge of the dangers, but, nevertheless, the choice is our own.

But loud noise for fun cannot always be confined only to those who choose to hear it. We may have the right to inflict noise damage on ourselves, but we have no right to damage other people against their wills. We have no right to allow the noises we make to spill out over others, endangering their hearing, their physical well-being, and their mental stability. If they react with violence, we have only ourselves to blame.

A conflict between makers of noise and unwilling listeners has arisen in recent years over recreational vehicles like snowmobiles, trail bikes, and motor boats. Each of these machines provides an effortless way for people to get away from roads and to enter undeveloped wilderness areas where wildlife has been undisturbed by modern society. But each of these machines is also very noisy. Each brings the uproar of modern life into the wilderness itself, driving birds from their nests, deer from the protective cover of thickets, and beaver from their lodges. These and many, many other animals have their natural way of life upset by our noisy recreation. People are upset too. Those who love the wilderness for its peace and tranquillity and who make the effort to enjoy it silently by hiking or canoeing become fiercely resentful of the invading hordes on their noisy machines.

Advertising for snowmobiles is designed to appeal to modern man's love of adventure and his fascination with the wilderness. But when snowmobiles invade wilderness areas, they disturb the natural environment with their noise.

As the problem grows, state and national park administrators are beginning to control the use of snowmobiles, motor bikes, and trail bikes in wilderness areas. But many regulations are still in the discussion stage and are being contested by the manufacturers and distributors of the machines. It is inevitable that people who want to enter wilderness areas the easy way will outnumber those who are willing to make a hard physical effort. But somehow we have to find a way of getting into the wilderness without taking with us the noise and stink of gasoline engines, which will lead to the destruction of the very beauty we have come to enjoy.

5

Quiet Please!

If we, our children, and our children's children are going to remain sane and healthy, it is vitally important that we find ways to control the crescendo of noise which is filling our world. How can we feel secure in our homes if they can be shaken apart by sonic booms? How can we protect ourselves from the unheard and deadly effects of infrasound? Who will be able to enjoy the excitement of loud hard rock if people of later generations are born deaf? It is tempting to believe that such possibilities of noise damage belong only to the fantasy world of science fiction. But our knowledge of existing technology and of human evolution tells us that they are real.

What can we do to defend ourselves against such dangers? First, we must *believe* that noise is dangerous. We must accept the fact that it is a harmful pollutant. This is not easy to do, because unwelcome facts are always hard to accept, especially when they affect us personally. It is easier to believe that the neighbor's snowmobile makes a dangerously loud noise than it is to believe that the noise from our own sports car is damaging; that *our* stereo is acceptable while *their* dishwasher is not. All of us must look at the facts unblinkingly and try not to let them become distorted by our personal likes and dislikes.

Once we accept the fact that noise is dangerous, we must learn all we can about the problem from many different sources. What kind of damage does noise cause? How is the damage done? How can it be prevented or controlled? We must then share our knowledge with others, helping to build up a massive and effective movement which can influence our elected representatives and get them to pass strong noise control laws.

As we have seen, the problem of noise pollution is not a new one. As long ago as 1907, Nobel Prize winner Dr. Robert Koch predicted: "The day will come when man will have to fight merciless noise as the worst enemy of his health." In 1937 the American Medical Association declared that "the multiple and insidious ill effects of noise constitute an inadequately recognized baneful influence on the lives of millions of persons throughout the country." (In other words, the many and sneaky effects of noise are bad for us, and we don't realize it.) Yet, despite these warnings, the volume of noise in the United States is still growing. In metropolitan areas it is twice as loud now as it was 15 years ago. Experts estimate that the volume will double again in the next 10 years.

Noise abatement laws have very slowly been appearing on the statute books. In 1948, the New York Court of Appeals made a landmark decision when it awarded

Matthew Slawinski, a drop forge worker, $1,661.25 in compensation for losing a large portion of his hearing because of noise at the plant where he worked. Three years later this decision was reinforced by a similar one in Wisconsin, in which another drop forge worker was awarded $1,575.00 for loss of hearing. Both cases set precedents for loss of hearing to be treated as an occupational disease for which compensation must be made. This principle is now accepted in 39 states.

In 1968 Congress called for a national aircraft noise abatement program. Since then the Federal Aviation Administration has been working with the aircraft industry to develop standards which will become obligatory. All new aircraft now being built will have to conform to regulations setting maximum noise levels at 108 effective perceived decibels (equivalent to about 96 decibels) when measured at one mile from the threshold of the runway, three and a half miles from the start of the take-off run, and 1,500 feet from the side of the runway. The noise may go up to 110 EPdBs at any one time, as long as this increase is offset by operating below the 108-EPdB standard for an equivalent time. The National Aeronautics and Space Administration has provided a $50 million subsidy for research and development on a new generation of quieter aircraft engines.

As was mentioned earlier, New York and California have state laws setting maximum levels of noise which may be made by vehicles on the highways. But neither state has provided the equipment or the people to enforce these laws effectively. Most truck owners find it cheaper to pay the rare $5 or $10 fine for violation of the noise ordinances than to suppress the noise their vehicles make.

At the level of city government, laws regulating the volume of noise which may disturb our lives vary greatly from place to place. Most of the laws that do exist are covered under the nuisance ordinances. Memphis, Tennessee, however, has maintained its distinguished record of noise control ever since 1937, when a vigorous antinoise campaign was begun by the editor of one of the city's leading newspapers. Specific noise abatement laws have been passed and are enforced by the police, who carry sound level meters. A $50 fine is imposed for exceeding the noise levels set by the city ordinances. But even in quiet-conscious Memphis, a building contractor can get

Memphis police measure traffic noise with a sound level meter. The city's tradition of quiet is so well established that serious violations of the noise ordinances are rare.

permission to extend his noisy operations into the night hours if he can show that he would suffer "loss or inconvenience" if confined to daylight hours of construction.

Chicago has a number of ordinances to control noise, but many of them are worded so vaguely that they are extremely difficult to enforce. Theoretically, there are controls on noise levels in the streets between certain hours; zones of quiet are set up around hospitals and schools; and zoning laws require industries not to exceed noise levels of 79 decibels measured at the boundaries of their plants. But in Chicago, as in so many other cities, public pressure has not yet become strong enough to guarantee that these laws will be enforced.

Some of the many environmental protection and anti-pollution groups forming all over the country are concentrating specifically on noise abatement. Best known of these organizations is Citizens for a Quieter City in New York. Chicago has a group called Citizens Against Noise. Cambridge, Massachusetts, has its Citizens League Against the Sonic Boom. Many environmental groups, such as the Minnesota Environmental Control Citizens Association, have special task forces on noise. The U. S. Public Health Service has an office for National Noise Study, and the Department of Transportation has an Office of Noise Abatement. On the international level, the International Association Against Noise operates from Zurich, Switzerland. Noise abatement work is also done by the World Health Organization, the Council of Europe, and the United Nations. The problem of noise pollution is truly worldwide, but the people who are prepared to spend time and energy fighting the menace of noise are still far too few.

Noise pollution won't kill you.
It can only drive you nuts or make you deaf.

There's so much noise in this city that you'd hardly think there's a need to advertise it.

Noise, after all, is something New Yorkers work with, eat with, try to sleep with, and wake up with—usually when they don't want to.

New York's noise is so pervasive that, except for those few noises loud enough to make themselves heard above the general din, it's usually taken for granted. And it shouldn't be.

Noise is dangerous.

If you think about it, you'll realize that most of the dangerous things in this world are noisy.

A gunshot is dangerous. It's also noisy.

Breaking glass is noisy. It's also dangerous.

As a result, you instinctively react to noise as a warning of danger. And living with the noise in New York is like having someone fire off a pistol behind your back 24 hours a day.

But while consciously you may be blasé about noise, your body, your nervous system and your subconscious are naive enough to keep right on reacting to it.

It can drive you nuts.

Loud, unexpected noises are very good at creating emotional stress. When the noise is continual—as it is in New York—so is the stress.

And continual emotional stress, as many psychiatrists believe, is enough to turn a normal adult, with normal problems, into a neurotic—if not an out-and-out psychotic.

In Ohio, for example, a scientist was so maddened by Air Force bombers flying over his house in the middle of the night that he tried to shoot them down with a rifle.

And in Japan, the noise from a pile-driver made a college student find some peace and quiet by sticking his head between the pile and the descending hammer.

If you've been living in the city for a number of years and you haven't gone off the deep end yet, you're still not off

the hook. Because if New York's noise pollution hasn't affected your mind, it's probably affecting your hearing.

It can make you deaf.

Ever since the last century, when blacksmiths and boilermakers started complaining to doctors about their hearing, the medical profession has known that noise can produce deafness.

Today, subway conductors, jackhammer operators and factory workers, to mention just a few, earn their living at the risk of their hearing. Unfortunately, millions who don't work in these occupations are subjected to the same occupational hazards.

Portable air compressors on New York streets are loud enough to drown out dynamite blasts.

Food blenders in our kitchens are actually louder than Niagara Falls.

Power mowers and poorly-muffled motorcycles are so noisy, they make factories seem like libraries.

As the noise gets louder and louder, the people who have to live with it get deafer and deafer. It used to be that people didn't start to lose their hearing until the age of 70. In big cities today, people start going deaf at 30.

If we don't solve the noise pollution problem now, in a few years it could automatically solve itself. By making us all too deaf to hear it.

Nobody ever does anything about anything unless people demand it.

In a big city like ours, individuals with legitimate complaints are dismissed as nuts, lunatics and crackpots.

But if enough "nuts", "lunatics" and "crackpots" get together, there's no telling what they can accomplish.

In Westchester, enough people were sick and tired of having their sleep interrupted by trucks with roaring exhausts to get a noise limit set on the New York State Thruway.

In Florida, enough people were bugged by noisy electrical appliances to get a law passed against them.

And in New York, enough people were infuriated by the noise they had to live with in their apartments to get at least some soundproofing written into a new Building Code.

But while there are enough concerned people to get some of New York's noise shut out of future apartments, there are still far too few to get it shut up for good. That's why there's such a thing as the Citizens for a Quieter City.

Your financial support is welcome. Your moral support is essential.

Citizens for a Quieter City needs your money to make people aware that the problem of noise pollution exists. And that it doesn't exist as something to be passively accepted as an inevitable burden of the human condition.

Your money will also help stimulate research on the problem and its solution.

But what's even more important to us than your money is your name.

With the names of twenty or fifty or a hundred thousand New Yorkers who are as outraged by noise as we are, we can prove that this city has had all the noise pollution it's going to take.

So please fill out the coupon. And don't feel embarrassed about sending it in without any money. A lot of people's names add up to more help to us than a few people's money. Because the one thing we can't afford to do about noise pollution is keep quiet about it.

Newspaper advertisement published by Citizens for a Quieter City

Welcome help has been given by the Ford Foundation, which has made a two-year, $300,000 grant to Citizens for a Quieter City, for experimental work in reducing noise in a six-block area of New York City. Organizers of the project plan to acquaint people in the area with the dangers of noise and with the methods of noise reduction. They will set up a noise complaint center and will seek the cooperation of government and industry in their work.

Although noise is already affecting the quality of life in sparsely populated parts of the country, its worst stresses are felt in the metropolitan areas. In these large communities served by busy highways and airports, people live close together, victims of the noise produced by the increasingly complex technology of city and suburban life. Population trends show that people continue to migrate from the country to the cities in the United States, so it is vitally important that city life be made as civilized as possible. One of the ways to do this is to cut down the pollution from noise which causes so much stress and ill health.

The acoustic anarchy that exists now is dangerous and costly. It damages human health and happiness, affects the well-being of other living creatures, and destroys inanimate objects. Surely it is high time that modern man learned to use his technology for the good of mankind and the preservation of the world in which he lives. As taxpayers we spend money on silent engines for submarines. Yet we say we cannot afford silent engines for the garbage trucks which pollute our streets with noise.

To create conditions under which we can live close together in harmony, we are going to have to change our priorities. When we have changed our own way of thinking and have banded together with like-minded people, we must then speak up and get our legislators to understand that their priorities must be changed as well. An attitude of mind that refuses to accept noise as inevitable can work wonders. We can all take heart from the action of a slim New York mother who stormed out of her house at eight o'clock one evening to rage at six burly workmen who were ripping up the street and keeping her child awake. To her amazement the men beamed at her. "Thanks, lady," said the foreman. "I was afraid we were going to be here all night. Our orders were to keep working until someone complained."

Noise is not inevitable. We can fight it, and we can win. The victory will not be quick and it will not be easy. But the sooner we start, the sooner we will get results.

Glossary

acoustic fatigue.   Structural weakness in material things caused by sound vibrations.

cochlea.   The snail-shaped structure in the inner ear which contains the organ of hearing.

decibel.   The unit used to measure sound intensity.

frequency.   The number of times a sound wave vibrates in a second. Sound frequency is measured in cycles per second, or in units called *hertz*, after the 19th-century German physicist Heinrich Hertz. One hertz is equal to one cycle per second.

infrasound.   Sound vibrating at frequencies too low to be heard by the human ear.

intensity.   The amount of energy flowing in a sound wave. A vibrating object transfers the energy of its movement to the air molecules around it. As the molecules push against other molecules, they pass the energy along in the form of a pressure wave.

loudness.   The strength of the sensation which a sound wave produces on the human ear and brain. Loudness depends on the intensity of the sound and on its pitch, as well as on other factors such as distance from the source of sound.

natural resonance frequency.   The frequency at which an object would vibrate if set in motion by some disturbance.

pitch. The highness or lowness of a sound. Pitch is determined by the frequency of a sound wave—the speed with which it vibrates. The faster the vibrations, the higher the pitch of the sound.

sonic boom. The loud noise produced when an object moves faster than the speed of sound. An aircraft flying at supersonic speeds builds up a shock wave of compressed air which surrounds the plane and trails behind it. When the trailing edge of the shock wave reaches the ground, it produces the sonic boom.

sympathetic vibrations. Vibrations in an object caused by a sound vibrating at the object's natural resonance frequency.

ultrasound. Sound vibrating at frequencies too high to be heard by the human ear. Ultrasound has many practical uses in industry and medicine.

Index

acoustic fatigue, 38-39
airports, 61-63, 64-66
appliances, 41-42, 44
automobiles, 52-57

buses, 58-59

Citizens for a Quieter City
(NYC), 47, 72, 89, 91
cochlea, 21, 25
Comet jet, 39
cookie cutter, 73-74
cycles per second, 14

decibel scale, 15-17

ear, anatomy of, 21-22, 25
eardrum, 21, 26
ear protectors, 44, 74-75, 81

Federal Aviation Administration
(FAA), 63, 64-65, 87
frequency, 13-14, 15, 20

garbage cans, 45-46

hair cells, 22, 24, 25
hearing: damage to, caused by
noise, 24, 26-28, 77; mechanism of, 21-22, 25
helicopters, 67-68

infrasound, 21
intensity, 15

jackhammer, 8, 72-73
jet aircraft, 63-64

legislation, noise control, 50, 61,
78-80, 86-89
Los Angeles International
Airport, 65-66
loudness, 15

Mabaan tribe, 28-29, 30
Mach number, 18

mass transit, 59
Memphis, Tenn., 50, 88-89
motorcycles, 57-58
mufflers, 53-54, 57-58
music, 10, 26-28, 34-35, 81, 82

natural resonance frequency, 38
noise: definition of, 8; effect of,
on animals, 36-37; effect of, on
mental and emotional health,
33-36, 43, 78; physical damage
caused by, 29, 31-32, 78; and
sleep, 32-33

Occupational Safety and Health
Act of 1970, 79-80
O'Hare Airport (Chicago), 62
organizations, antinoise, 47, 72, 89

pitch, 13-14

roadways, 59, 61

sirens, 49
snowmobiles, 83-84
sonar, 20
sonic boom, 18-20, 37, 40, 68-70
sound: characteristics of, 13-15;
nature of, 11-12; speed of, 18
sound level meter, 15
soundproofing: in factories, 80;
in homes, 47-48
SST, 68
sympathetic vibrations, 38

tires, 55-56
trail bikes, 83-84
trucks, 58-59

ultrasound, 20

Walsh-Healey Public Contracts
Act, 78-79, 81
workmen's compensation for
hearing loss, 76-77, 87

95

About the Authors

Pollution: The Noise We Hear is one of eight books on pollution written by Claire Jones, Steve J. Gadler, and Paul H. Engstrom. This volume was a cooperative effort, each person contributing his or her own knowledge and experience, with the final result a kind of "literary synergism."

Paul H. Engstrom is a minister, a lawyer, and a family counselor, as well as president and cofounder of the Minnesota Environmental Control Citizens' Association. Under his leadership, MECCA has worked for preservation of Lake Superior and the Mississippi watershed, reduction of radioactive pollution, reuse of materials in solid waste, and many other environmental goals to improve the quality of life. Thus Rev. Engstrom's major contribution to this series of books on pollution was a social and legal perspective resulting from direct experience.

Steve J. Gadler also is experienced in the fight to save the environment; he is a registered professional engineer who was an environmentalist long before pollution became a national issue. A retired Air Force Colonel, Mr. Gadler has for many years been asking pertinent, revealing questions about the damage caused by our industrial society. He has been especially concerned about radioactivity, which is an invisible but deadly threat to life itself. In 1967, the governor of Minnesota appointed him as a member of the state's Pollution Control Agency. Mr. Gadler's technical expertise is apparent in each book in the series.

Claire Jones is an experienced writer who first became aware of the dangers of pollution in 1956, when she lived through one of the famous London killer smogs. Teaming up with Rev. Engstrom and Mr. Gadler gave her an excellent way to express her concern over the condition of the environment. However, her contribution has been more than a concerned citizen's point of view and a crisp, sparkling writing style. A native of England, Mrs. Jones brings a special international outlook to this series. None of the problems of pollution can be seen as less than worldwide, and this important perspective gives *The Noise We Hear* added value.